T0368648

Moonlit Messages

Aisha Abdi

Moonlit Messages

© 2024 Aisha Abdi. All rights reserved.

No part of this book may be reproduced, stored in a retrieval system, or transmitted by any means without the written permission of the author.

AuthorHouse™
1663 Liberty Drive
Bloomington, IN 47403
www.authorhouse.com
Phone: 833-262-8899

Because of the dynamic nature of the Internet, any web addresses or links contained in this book may have changed since publication and may no longer be valid. The views expressed in this work are solely those of the author and do not necessarily reflect the views of the publisher, and the publisher hereby disclaims any responsibility for them.

Any people depicted in stock imagery provided by Getty Images are models, and such images are being used for illustrative purposes only.
Certain stock imagery © Getty Images.

This book is printed on acid-free paper.

ISBN: 979-8-8230-3675-7 (sc)
ISBN: 979-8-8230-3676-4 (e)

Library of Congress Control Number: 2024922849

Print information available on the last page.

Published by AuthorHouse 12/26/2024

authorHOUSE®

This book is dedicated to my

daughter, Rayanna.

Raya is a little girl who resides in a small house located in an estate surrounded by huge trees and the night sky. Her days were full of joy and affection, spent with her grandmother. Raya's mother was motivated by the dreams of education in the USA. Despite the geographical distance between them, the love of a mother and her daughter could not be severed.

Each evening, when the moon was up and the twin stars painted the sky, Raya and her grandmother would sit by the window and watch the night. Raya understood that her mother was far away, but the stars and the moon in the sky had a different story to tell.

5

Although Raya's mom was far away, their connection remained strong. As Raya's mom got lost looking at the sky, she, too would send her love across the great expanse.

It was in this nightly custom, that Raya and her mom found solace. Their actions, a silent exchange of "I love you" were painted in the moonlit sky, like moonlight messages.

Each morning, Raya would wake up early to check if her mother had sent any special clouds her way. Grandmother taught her that some clouds carried wishes, and Raya was certain the heart-shaped ones were from Mommy.

During video calls, Raya would press her tiny hands against the screen. She would imagine that felt her mommy's warmth through the phone. She would say, "Mommy, I touched the same moon you touched last night," with her eyes twinkling with joy.

When Raya really missed her mommy, her grandmother would help her write letters to the stars. This became a tradition where they would fold paper airplanes and release them from their window. Raya would wish upon the stars that the night breeze would carry her words across the great ocean to her mom.

13

Every night before bed, Raya would whisper her secrets to her favorite doll. This was the doll her mom gave her before she left. She would say, "Please visit Mommy in her dreams. Let her know I am being brave and cannot wait to see her again."

On special nights, especially when the stars seemed to shine their brightest, Raya would listen to her grandmother's stories about her mother's childhood. These stories made Raya giggle. She could not believe her mommy was once small like her. It was such stories that helped her feel like her mother was right there, sharing in their laughter under the same starlit sky.

17

It was these moonlit messages that grew to be a tale of love that defied distance.

They helped prove that despite where life takes us, the heart's murmurs can be heard across seas and continents, connecting the heart of a mother, daughter, and grandmother under the watchful eye of the moon and the silence of the night.

Printed in the United States
by Baker & Taylor Publisher Services